JOKES FOR MOM

TERRIBLY GOOD JOKES FOR MOM

Printed Worldwide
First Printing, 2018

1. Why is braille easy to learn?

a. Because you just need to get a feel for it

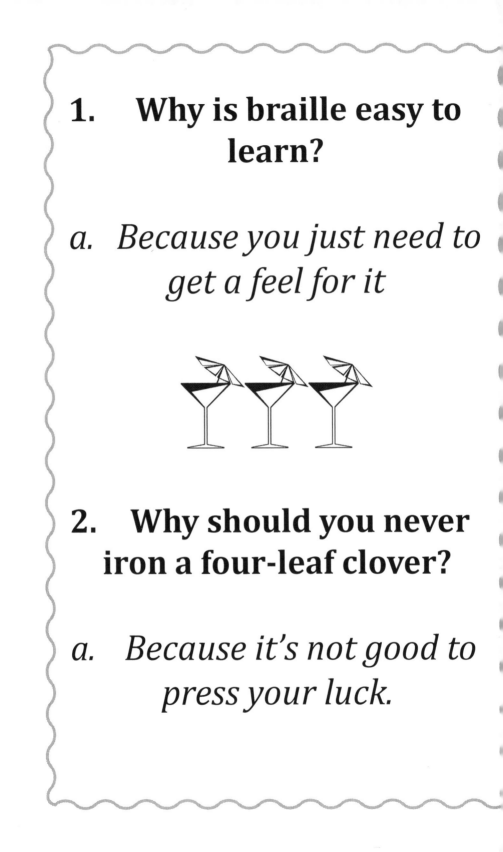

2. Why should you never iron a four-leaf clover?

a. Because it's not good to press your luck.

3. **What is the leading cause of dry skin?**

a. *Towels.*

4. **How illiterate am I?**

a. *So illiterate that I can't put it into words.*

5.   Why did my little brother's tummy hurt at bedtime?

a.   Because he ate a clock.

6.   What do you call it when someone can always find where Indian bread is?

a.   Naan-sense.

7.   What is the one thing that flat-earthers are afraid of?

a.   Sphere itself.

8.   Why did the plastic surgeon have to get a box of tissues?

a.   Because he picked so many people's noses.

9.   What do you call deaf bears?

a.   *B.*

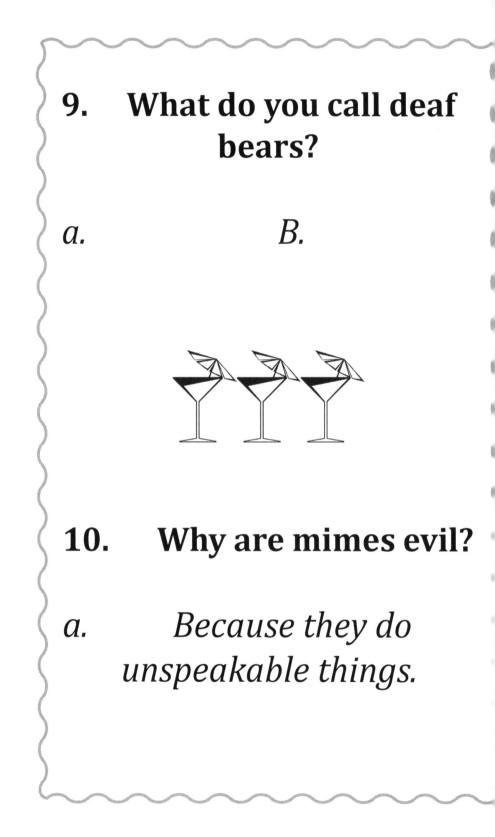

10.   Why are mimes evil?

a.   *Because they do unspeakable things.*

11.   How does a circle make friends at a bar?

a.   He buys everyone a round.

12.   What's the best way to leave your job as a stage designer?

a.   By making a scene.

13. **What's the best part of a party joke?**

a. *The punch line.*

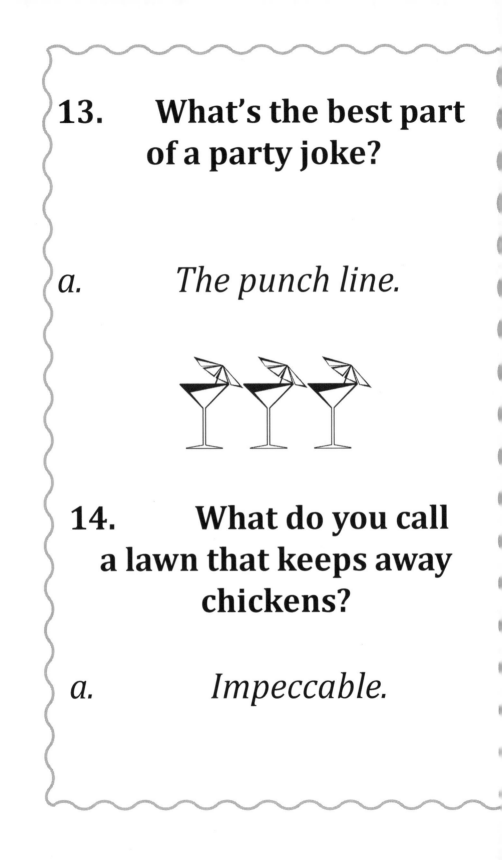

14. **What do you call a lawn that keeps away chickens?**

a. *Impeccable.*

15.   Why does an airline luggage worker not make a good lawyer?

a.   Because the're always losing cases.

16.   What do you tell a selfish moon?

a.   The world doesn't revolve around you!

17. **Why is a broken website like an injured tennis player?**

a. *Because its servers are always down.*

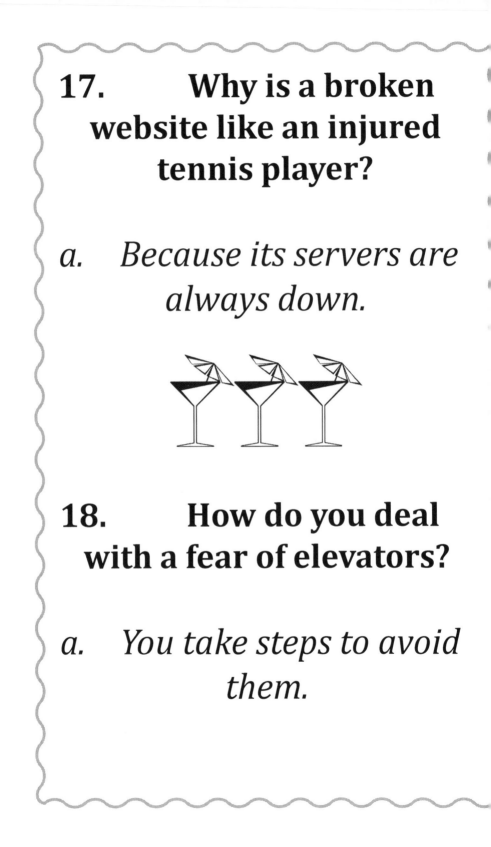

18. **How do you deal with a fear of elevators?**

a. *You take steps to avoid them.*

19.   **How do you turn root beer into beer?**

a.   *Put it into a square cup.*

20.   **Why did the scientist talk to himself?**

a.   *Because he finally developed cloning!*

21. **What grade did the Canadian get on the test?**

a. *An Eh plus.*

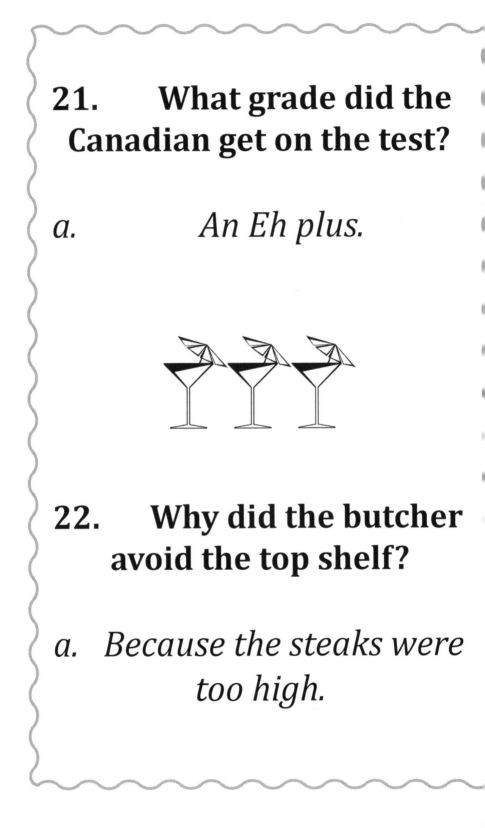

22. **Why did the butcher avoid the top shelf?**

a. Because the steaks were too high.

23. **How do you cut the ocean in half?**

a. *By using a seasaw.*

24. **Why do socialists only write in lowercase?**

a. *Because they hate capitalism.*

25.   What is the best way to travel the flat earth?

a.   On a plane.

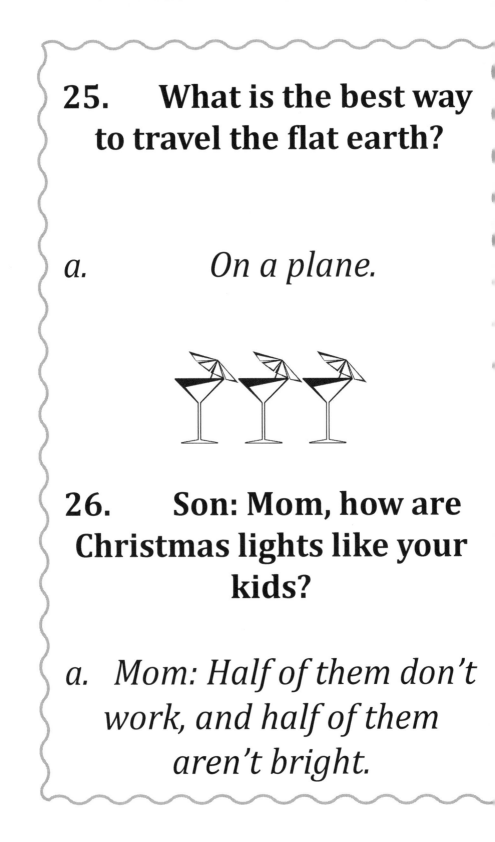

26.   Son: Mom, how are Christmas lights like your kids?

a. Mom: Half of them don't work, and half of them aren't bright.

27. **What did the pirate say when he turned 80-years-old?**

a.   *Aye matey!*

28. **What do you write on a pot of boiling water's gravestone?**

a.   *She will be mist.*

29.   Son: Mom, I want to date this vegetarian I met online!

a.   Mom: Why? You've never met herbivore.

30.   What happens to punctuation when they commit crimes?

a.   They get sentenced.

31. **Why did the prosecutors make the criminal say a tongue twister?**

a. *Because they were seeking a tough sentence.*

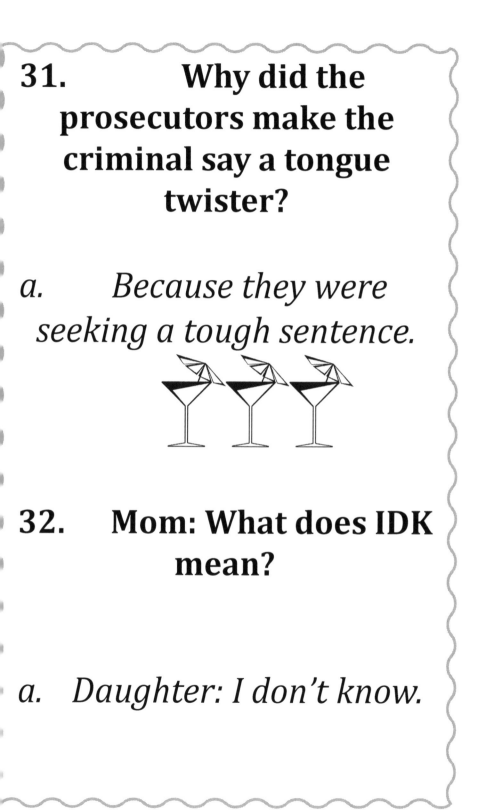

32. **Mom: What does IDK mean?**

a. *Daughter: I don't know.*

33.   Did you hear about the guy who was addicted to the Hokey Pokey?

a.   *He was able to turn himself around.*

34.   I would like to thank you, student loans.

a.   *I don't think I'll ever be able to repay you.*

35. **Why did the astronaut break up with his girlfriend before blasting off?**

a. *Because he needed space.*

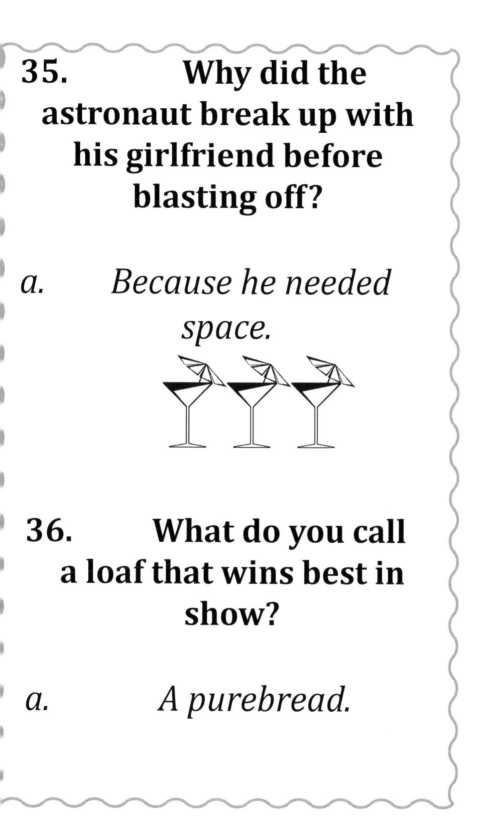

36. **What do you call a loaf that wins best in show?**

a. *A purebread.*

37. **What did the mom name her daughter with one leg shorter than the other?**

a. *Eileen.*

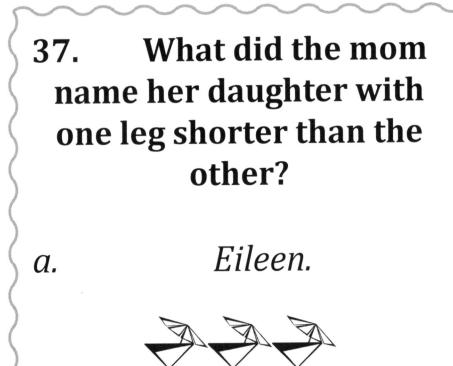

38. **Why is sleeping so easy?**

a. *Because you can do it with your eyes closed.*

39. **What do you call it when King Midas's dog touches a phone?**

a. *A golden receiver.*

40. **How often do chemists make pun?**

a. *Periodically.*

41.   Why did the dog try to communicate with the tree?

a.   Because it had bark.

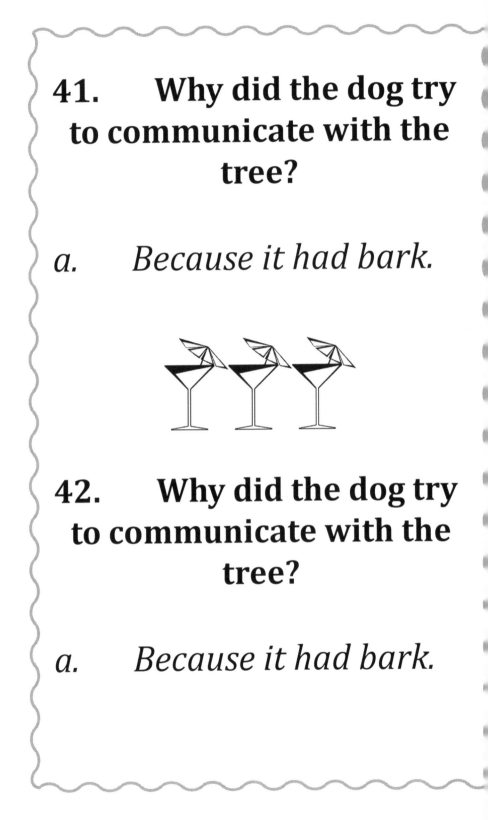

42.   Why did the dog try to communicate with the tree?

a.   Because it had bark.

43.   Why did the golfer's mom sew his pants?

a.   Because he got a hole in one.

44.   What do you call a fish with three eyes?

a.   A fiiish.

45.   **Why did the cow have no money?**

a.   *Because the farmer milked her dry.*

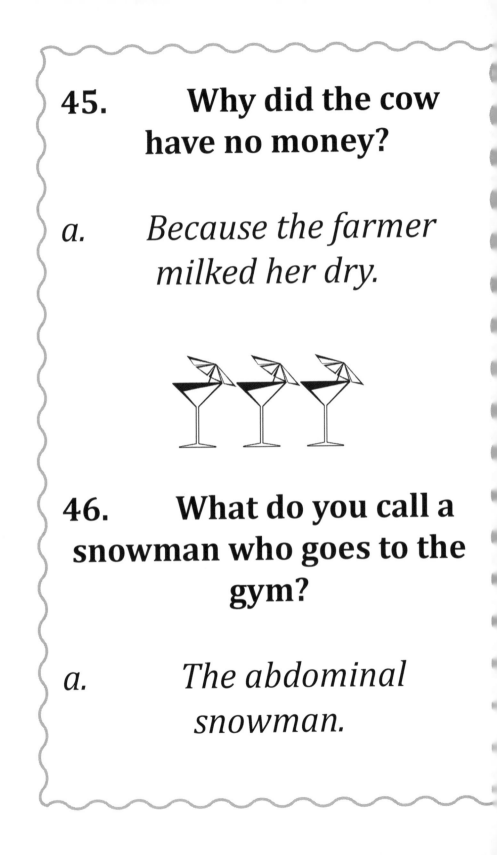

46.   **What do you call a snowman who goes to the gym?**

a.   *The abdominal snowman.*

47.   What country are French fries really from?

a.   Greece.

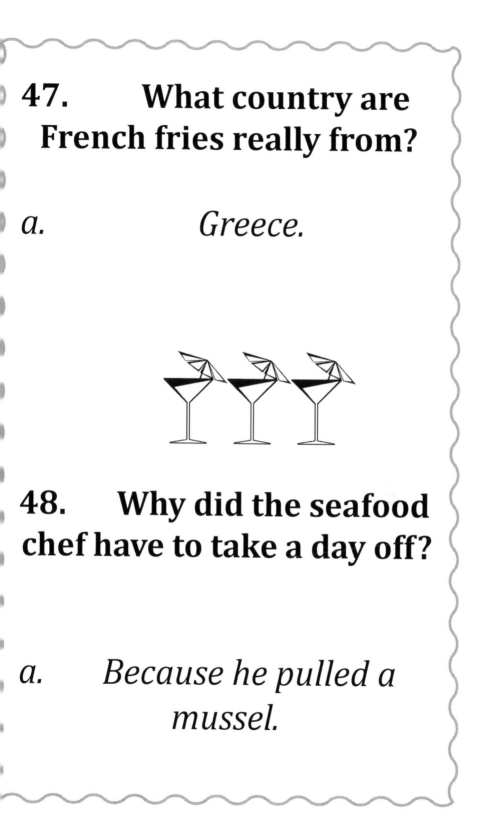

48.   Why did the seafood chef have to take a day off?

a.   Because he pulled a mussel.

49.   Why did the camper go to a therapist?

a. Because she was feeling tents.

50.   Why did the cannibal stop eating the clown?

a. Because it tasted funny.

51.   Why did mom decide to start inspecting mirrors?

a.   Because it was a job she could really see herself doing.

52.   What do you call a song about tortillas?

a.   A rap.

53. **Why did the slug go to the hospital?**

a. Because it was a-salted.

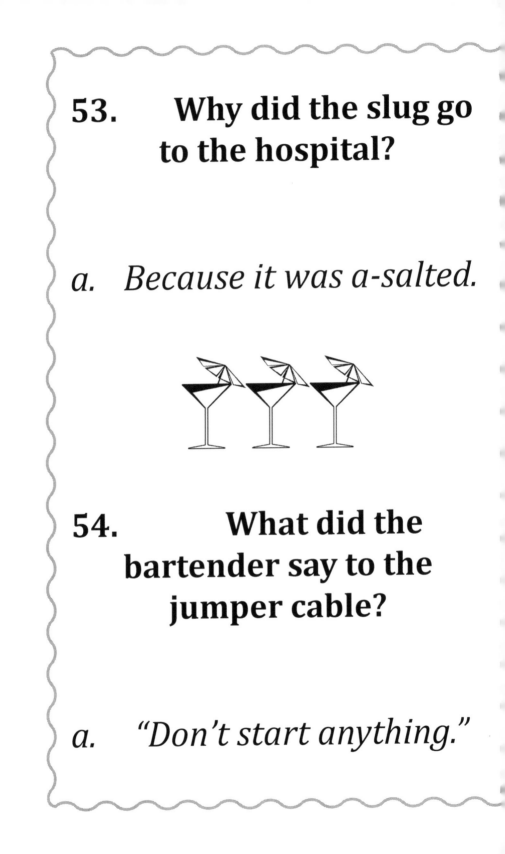

54. **What did the bartender say to the jumper cable?**

a. "Don't start anything."

55.   **Why did the crazy Parisian jump into the river?**

a.   *Because she was in Seine.*

56.   **What do you call a shopping center that's been passed down from generation to generation?**

a.   *Mall in the Family.*

57. **What letter do janitor's hate?**

a. *P.*

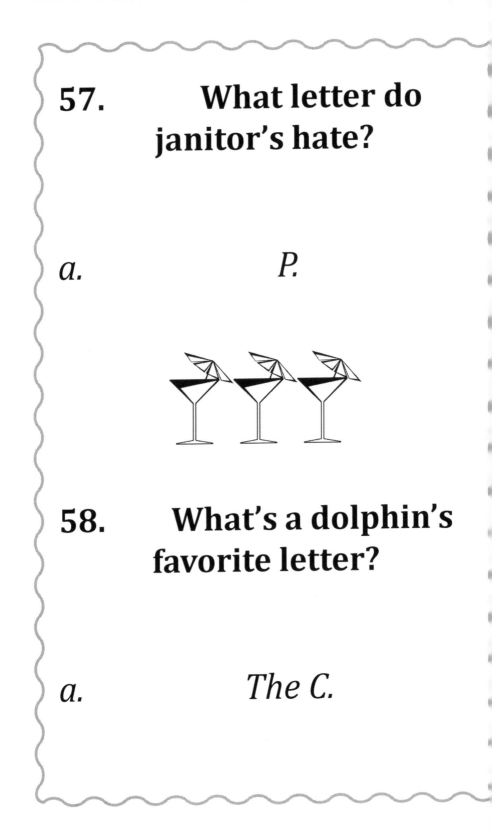

58. **What's a dolphin's favorite letter?**

a. *The C.*

59.   **Why do cows hate wearing flip flops?**

a.   *Because they lactose.*

60.   **What do you call a short psychic on the run from the cops?**

a.   *A small medium at large.*

61. **What the dough say to the rolling pin?**

a. *"You flatter me."*

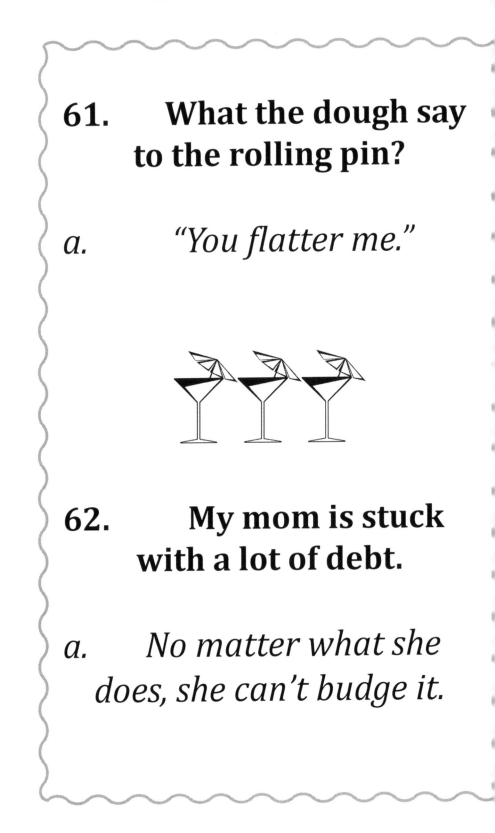

62. **My mom is stuck with a lot of debt.**

a. *No matter what she does, she can't budge it.*

63. **What key does a coal worker sing in?**

a.   *A miner.*

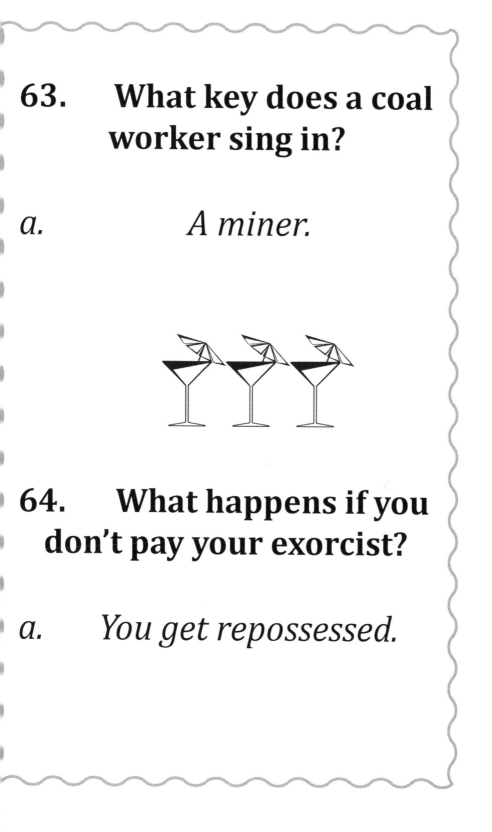

64. **What happens if you don't pay your exorcist?**

a.   *You get repossessed.*

65.   What do you call a group of singing cleaners?

a.   A soap opera.

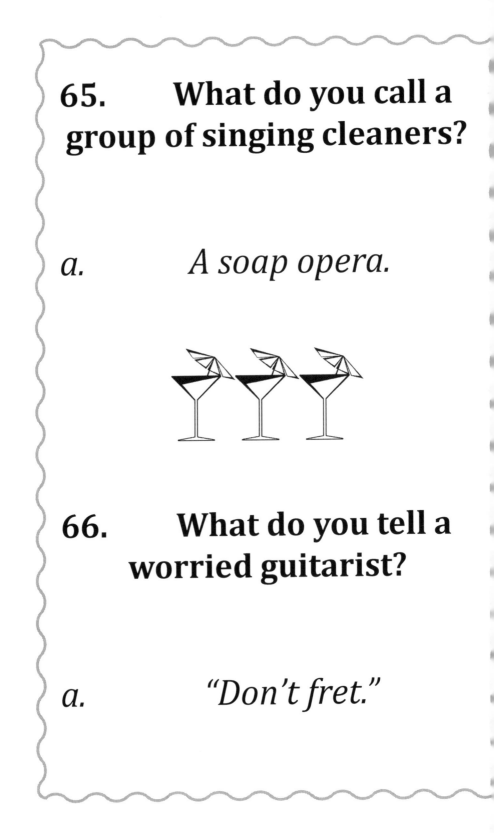

66.   What do you tell a worried guitarist?

a.   "Don't fret."

67.   Why did the bear stutter?

a.   He had big pause.

68.   Mom: Son, how come you only know 25 letters of the alphabet?

a.   Son: I don't know y.

69. How does Bambi start a Mother's Day card?

a. *"Deer Mom..."*

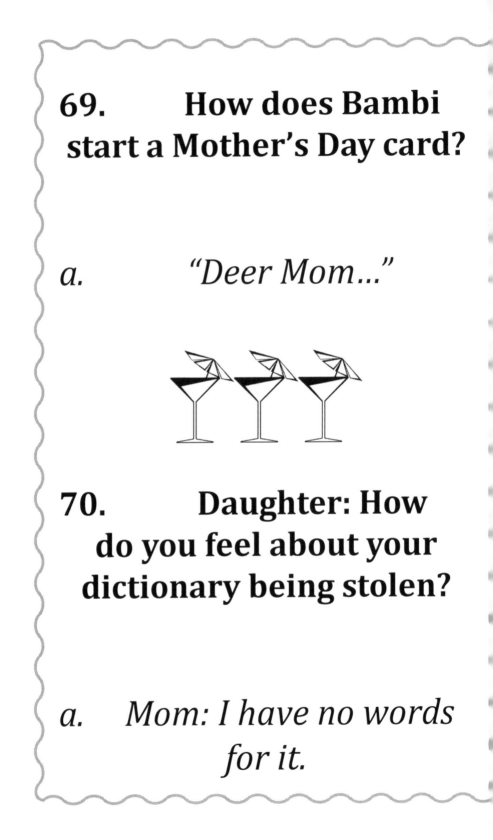

70. Daughter: How do you feel about your dictionary being stolen?

a. *Mom: I have no words for it.*

71.   Why is a bicycle unable to stand on its own?

a.   Because it's two-tired.

72.   When are male bugs able to float?

a.   When they're boy ant.

73.   What does a tightrope walker do at an ATM?

a.   She checks her balance.

74.   How did mom feel after she bleached her hair?

a.   She felt light-headed.

75.   Why should Winnie the Pooh avoid stepping on nails?

a.   Because he's bear-foot.

76.   Why are taxidermists so smart?

a. Because they know their stuff.

77.   **Why is the average so cruel?**

a.   *Because it's mean.*

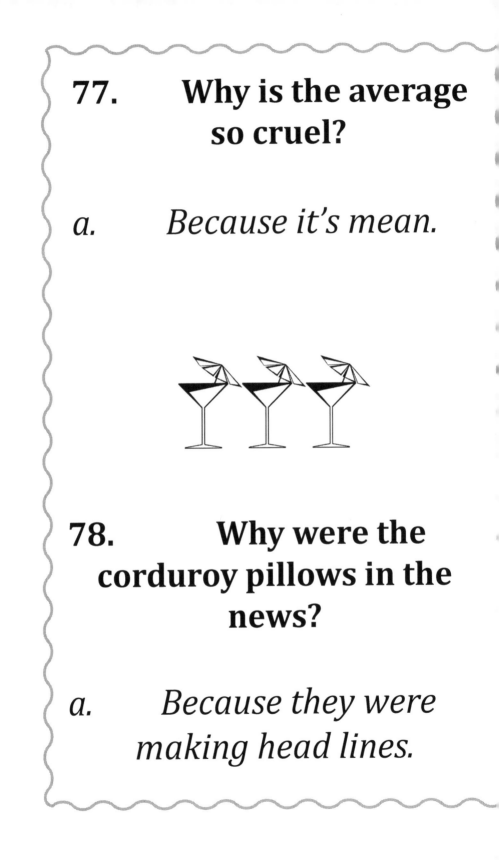

78.   **Why were the corduroy pillows in the news?**

a.   *Because they were making head lines.*

79. **Why did the lowercase letter leave work?**

a. *Because it was the end of his shift.*

80. **How do you kill an Easter Egg?**

a. *You dye it.*

81.   Son: Mom, could you make clocks for dinner?

a.   Mom: No, son, that's very time consuming.

82.   What do you call it when your mom marries a ladder?

a.   Your stepladder.

83.   **Why did the Mom fall into the hole?**

a.   *She couldn't see that well.*

84.   **Where do Pixar workers get tattoos?**

a.   *Monsters Ink.*

85.   **Son: Mom, what rhymes with orange?**

a.   *Mom: No it doesn't.*

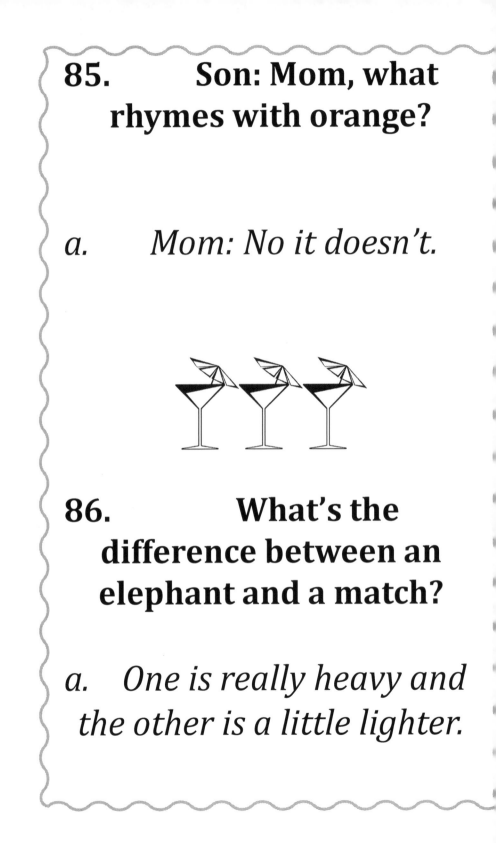

86.   **What's the difference between an elephant and a match?**

a.   *One is really heavy and the other is a little lighter.*

87. **Where do you print gossip?**

a. *At the rumor mill.*

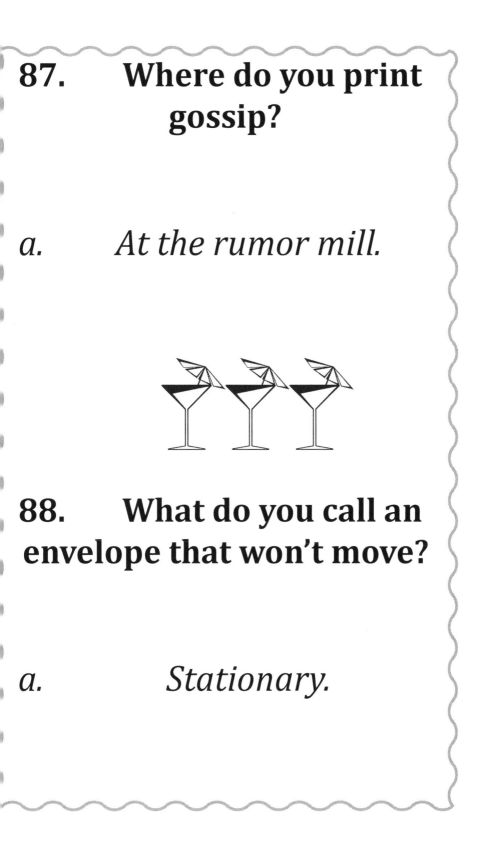

88. **What do you call an envelope that won't move?**

a. *Stationary.*

89.   My mom told me to stop impersonating a flamingo.

a.   So I had to put my foot down.

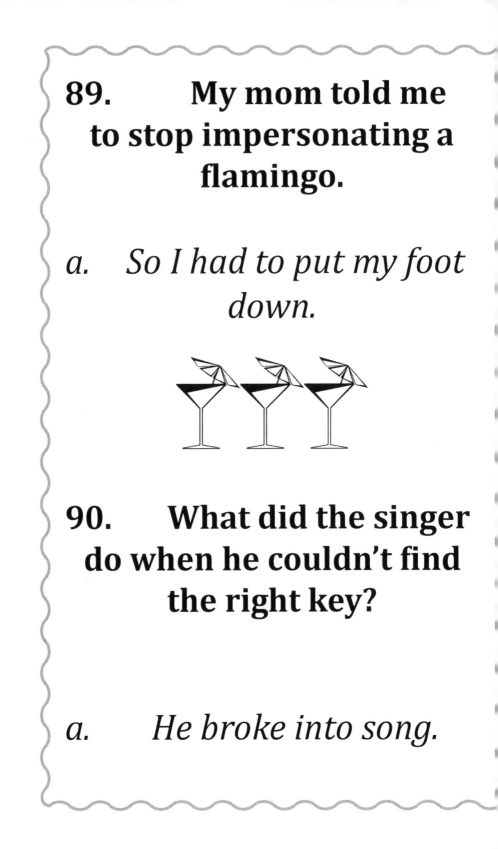

90.   What did the singer do when he couldn't find the right key?

a.   He broke into song.

91. **What do you use to tie your shoes in a spaceship?**

a. *Astronauts.*

92. **Why was the calendar close to death?**

a. *Because its days were numbered.*

93. **Daughter: Mom, I want to write a book on sharks.**

a. *Mom: Wouldn't paper be easier?*

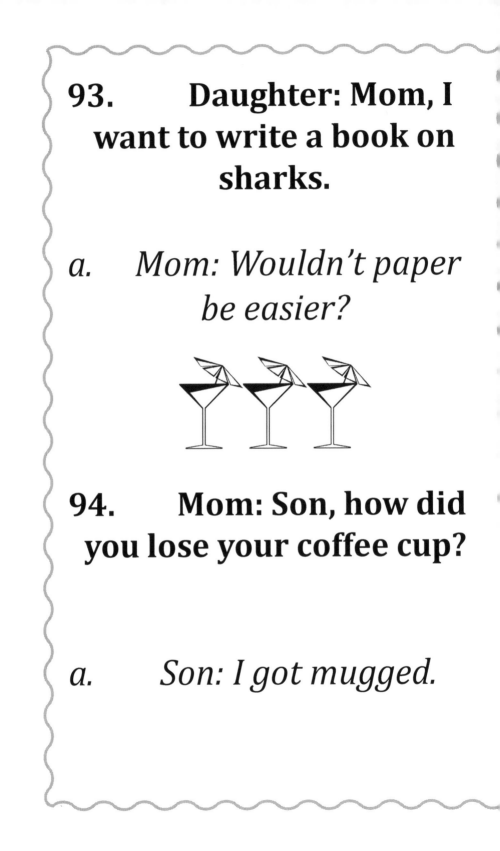

94. **Mom: Son, how did you lose your coffee cup?**

a. *Son: I got mugged.*

95.   How can you tell when eggs find you funny?

a.   When they crack up.

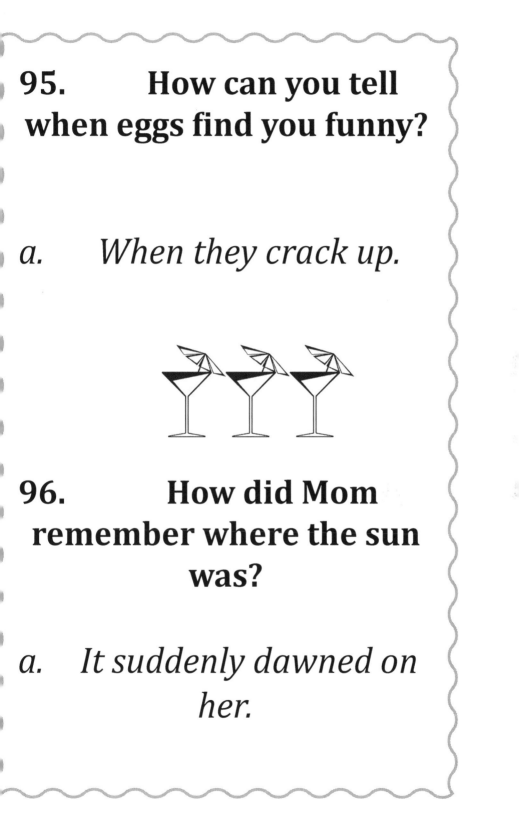

96.   How did Mom remember where the sun was?

a.   It suddenly dawned on her.

97.   What do you call a corkboard that doesn't fit with the décor?

a.   *Tacky.*

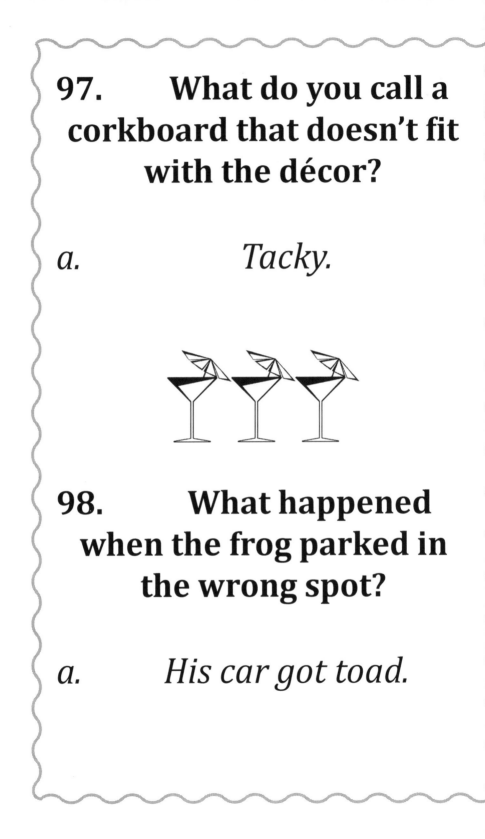

98.   What happened when the frog parked in the wrong spot?

a.   *His car got toad.*

99. **Why should you never believe anything atoms say?**

a. *Because they make up everything.*

100. **What do you call a dull pencil?**

a. *Pointless.*

Made in the USA
Monee, IL
11 April 2021